Written by Natanella Illouz-Eliaz
Illustrated by Imily Mitrani

@NatanellaE

Natanella Illouz-Eliaz

ISBN/SKU: 979-8-3303-8700-7

To my mother and father -

Thank you for giving me wings.

To Roy, Assif, and Eilon -

Thank you for supporting me in this journey.

NIE

To my mother who always believed in me. To Yuval, Ivri, and Gili - you are my inspiration for everything.

IM

Contents

Chapter 1: The Gift

It was a warm afternoon, and I was in my room reading *Wonder*, a book I really enjoy. I was so caught up in the story that I didn't notice my mom standing at the door. I was surprised when I suddenly felt her hand on my shoulder.

"Mom!" We laughed together and hugged. "I brought you a present, Lona," Mom said.

"What is it?" I asked curiously, and Mom answered, "Something you can take care of."

"Meet Arbi," Mom said. "Arbi was born right out of Mother Nature. She emerged out of a seed in the ground."

"She? You mean Arbi?" I asked. "Yes, our little Arbi," Mom smiled.

I took the little pot with Arbi in it and placed it on my desk.

Mom started to tell me about Arbi, "Plants like Arbi are called dicots because they have two leaves when they are born."

"Dicots? Why dicots?" I asked.

"Well, because they have two cotyledons. Cotyledons are the first leaves plants develop. Di means two.

There are also plants that are born with just one leaf. They are called monocots. Mono means one."

"Mom, are they really born?" I asked, because I didn't know that plants were *actually* born.

"No no, Lona. They are not actually born. Plants germinate. When they germinate they either have one or two first leaves. Sometimes they look different from what are called the true leaves. The true leaves are the leaves that develop after the cotyledons."

"Oh I see, like we have our baby teeth when we are young, but then we get adult teeth?" I tried to make sense of what Mom explained to me.

"Yes, dear, in a way you could think of it like that. Basically the cotyledons are the initial source of energy for the plant, before it can develop some true leaves."

I got more and more curious as I was learning new facts about plants, so I asked my mom to tell me something exciting.

"Something exciting..." Mom stopped to think for a few seconds. "Let's see, something I find exciting about plants is that between their two leaves hides a very precious part of the plant. This area of the plant is called the MERISTEM. The meristem is a group of cells from which all aerial organs that Arbi will make throughout her life will develop." My mom looked at me and tried to understand whether I was able to follow her.

I nodded, so my mom knew that I understood, and she could go on with her description.

Mom continued, "In order to guard this precious area, Arbi and all her fellow dicots emerge humbly out of the soil with their leaves turned down and a curved stem called the apical hook. This way, the meristem is protected when the seedling emerges through the soil to meet the sun."

THE APICAL HOOK

"Mom, is it called an apical hook, because at that stage the seedling has the shape of a hook?" I wondered.

"Yes, my dear, the stem below the leaves looks just like a hook at first.

I bet you realized by now that Arbi isn't just any plant.

"Arbi is an *Arabidopsis thaliana*, that is a MODEL plant," Mom told me, excited.

"A model plant?" I asked her. "What is a model plant?! Does it pose and smile to the camera?"

"No, Lona, of course not," my mom laughed hard, and she scrunched up her nose as if she was saying 'silly you'!

"So, what IS a model plant?" I insisted.

Chapter 2: A Model Plant

My mom was just about to start telling me about model plants when my sister, Eli, burst into my room.

"Eli, I thought you were already asleep," said Mom, quite surprised to see Eli wide awake and bubbly.

"After I finished my shower, Dad was organizing the garage, and I asked if I could help him. He was happy for me to help, so I stayed with him in the garage, handing him all kinds of things to put in place. Then I brushed my teeth, and now I'm ready for bed! Mom, come read me a story!" said Eli in one long sentence, and then took a huge breath of air when she finished.

"Come, my dear, you can join us and fall asleep on Lona's bed tonight." Mom looked at me to seek my confirmation. I was just happy that we could continue our conversation. Anyway, Eli always falls asleep in two seconds.

"A model plant is a plant used in science to learn about plants in general. Arbi - *Arabidopsis thaliana* is a model plant," Mom explained.

At this point, when my mom told me more about Arbi and her species, I was thinking to myself, "Why is this *Arabidopsis thaliana* a model plant? You probably had the same thought. I had never heard of that plant, even though my mom is a plant scientist.

"Mom, why is Arbi the model plant and not a cucumber plant? Or cherry tomatoes? They're really cute! And tasty too. They are also way more well-known. Everybody knows what a cucumber plant is! Oh, or a lemon tree! Lots of people in our neighborhood have lemon trees!"

Mom smiled at me. "Smart girl, you have great suggestions for model plants! Let me explain to you why Arbi is a model plant, and then you can decide if it is suitable to be a model. *Arabidopsis thaliana* was chosen as a model plant for three main reasons:

1. It's SMALL, which allows researchers to grow many plants in small rooms or growth chambers.

2. Each plant produces MANY SEEDS, so we always have more of them to play with.

3. It has a SMALL GENOME. The genome is almost like the *HOW TO* book, the instructions for making the plant."

"Do I have a genome like Arbi has?" I got curious about the instuction book to make - ME!

"Quite surprisingly all organisms have a genome, and it has the same components, or building blocks, in all organisms. Just four different letters A T G and C form endless combinations to create the marvelous diversity we have on our planet, like trees, whales, ants, and so much more. Some genomes are longer than others. Some genomes are more complex than others and have multiple copies. Arbi's genome is relatively simple and has just two copies. That means that we can learn about most of its genes relatively easily."

"Let me see if I understand, Mom. Arbi is a model plant, because it's small, makes many seeds, and what's the last thing? I forgot."

"Yes, you got two out of three!" said Mom. "The last thing was that it has a small genome. Every living thing, including us, has a genetic code. Arbi's code is relatively simple, which makes it easier for the scientists to study. We can learn the code, and then look at Arbi and try to understand parts of the instructions bit by bit." Mom yawned, and I wasn't sure who was going to fall asleep first - me or her.

" You know what else is really cool about Arbi? Well, really about plants in general?" Mom surprised me by being excited even when she was REALLY tired.

"What? Tell me!" I got enthusiastic easily.

"Think about us, humans. A baby is born with all its organs, ears, eyes, arms, and hands... Plants are different. They germinate with a rootlet and a small shoot with one or two leaves, but later in life they will develop many more leaves, flowers, and fruit. Do you remember how many leaves Arbi germinated with?" Mom asked me.

"Two!" I answered quickly, Mom was impressed.

"You are brilliant! Do you remember what plants with two leaves are called?"

I stopped to think a bit... but didn't quite remember. It was something like di... diy... diacon? No, no, that didn't sound right. "Mom, what are they called? I don't remember."

"Dicots," she said, "because they have two cotyledons, which are the first two leaves of the plant, already there in the plant embryo."

"Wait, Mom, what?? Plants have embryos?" I was surprised! I never thought of plants as little embryos or babies.

"Yes, my love, but I think we have learned so much for one day. It's time for bed now." Mom kissed me on the forehead and picked up sleeping Eli to put her in her own bed.

I stayed awake for a while imagining a plant embryo in its seed.

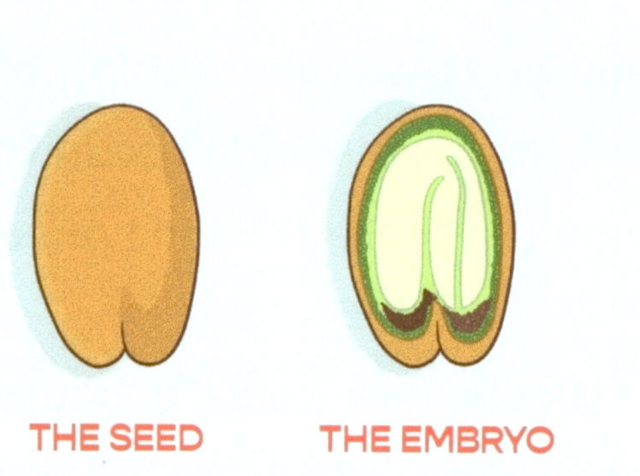

Chapter 3: Sharing is Caring

The next day after school, my mom and I took Cooper to meet his doggy friends at the park. Playing with his friends at the park was the highlight of Cooper's day, and it made me

happy to see him so joyful.

When we returned, my dad had already made dinner, and the table was set. Eli was helping Daddy cut the vegetables.

"Choose your three-colored vegetables," Dad said, as always.

I chose broccoli, red peppers, and carrots. My little sister, Eli, chose cucumbers, tomatoes, and carrots. We start every meal with vegetables before eating anything else. Usually, Mom or Dad prepares different vegetables that we like, so we have a variety to choose from. Sometimes, to make it interesting, they cut them up in different shapes, and Eli and I create our own vegetable mandala on our plate before eating.

If I'm being honest, my little sister's veggie

mandala is usually prettier than mine, but don't tell her I said that.

The next day at school, I was anxious to tell my best friend, Ruth, about Arbi and all the new cool stuff I learned. I assumed that nobody in my class knew any of this.

I started sharing with Ruth at lunch break, as we sat at a table outside. "Yesterday, my mom came home from work with a present just for me. She said it was something I could take care of, and at the beginning I thought it was another dog!" I opened my eyes wide, as I was trying to recreate the curiosity that sparked when my mom told me she brought me something.

"Well, was it a dog??" Ruth asked.

"No, it was a plant! A plant called Arbi," I answered.

"Oh," sighed Ruth, with a slight disappointment in her voice.

"I know, I know, it sounds lame. But actually, it was kind of cool," I insisted.

"Cool? Why was it cool?" asked Ruth.

"Well, it turns out that Arbi is a model plant." I looked at Ruth, and wondered if she might be interested in hearing more about Arbi or whether I should drop it.

"A MODEL plant, you said?" Now Ruth opened her eyes wide, and pushed her head forward with her chin leading the pose.

"OK, what is a MODEL plant?" asked Ruth. Every time she said model, she really emphasized the MO part. Suddenly I noticed that everybody around the table got quiet and was listening.

"A model plant means that it's a plant that scientists use as a model to learn things about plants in general. Like how they grow, how they make new organs, like flowers. You know, we are born with all our organs, like eyes and hands, but plants can grow new organs even as they grow older!"

Jonah jumped into the conversation and said, "Wow! It's like science fiction! Like I could grow a tail now!"

"Yes, yes!" I got carried away by his excitement.

"How do they do that?" Jordan asked.

"I don't really know yet, but there is an area in the plant called the meristem. From the meristem, all the new organs grow." I tried to recap what I just recently talked about with my mom.

"Me-ris-tem," some of them repeated together. It felt really good to share what I had learned and see them get excited. But as I was feeling a warmth in my heart generated by my friends' shared curiosity, a different voice rose up.

"Guys, seriously? This is like sooo boring. What are you, complete nerds?" Danny stood up holding his sandwich in his hand and spitting meanness out of his mouth.

My heart sank, and all the sparkles I had felt around my chest turned into small spikes. It was painful. Everybody was quiet. He always does this. Whenever we all agree on something, Danny comes to crash the party. I wanted to say something, but I couldn't bring myself to speak. I was afraid that now everybody thought I was boring.

All of a sudden Jonah said, "Danny, I guess you didn't get it, but plants are really cool. They don't JUST grow."

There was silence around the table. Then Jonah continued: “But you know, we don’t all have to like the same things. That’s fine.”

Still, a loud silence at the table. Only far away voices from the surrounding tables were heard in the background.

“And by the way,” added Ruth, “I think ‘nerd’ is a compliment, like ‘smart’, so yeah, thanks!”

I was feeling those spikes turning back into sparkles all across my chest. Danny just walked away, and we heard the whistle calling us to go back to class. We all organized our lunch boxes and returned to class together.

Chapter 4: Friendship

I love my friends so much, I thought. Throughout the whole lesson in school, I was thinking about how grateful I was for them talking back to Danny, and how good that made me feel.

I promised myself two things at that moment. One is that, if I would have the chance to speak up for someone else, I would be brave and do it, like my friends did for me. Second, I would let my friends know how grateful I was that they did that for me.

That evening after I took my shower and got into bed to read, I told my father and mother about what happened in school. My mother caressed my hair while they were listening to me. When I told them about the promise I made to myself and how I was too shy to actually do that, Dad asked, "Do you want us to suggest how you can get over being shy?"

"Of course!" I said, hopeful.

Dad suggested several things I could do. He suggested writing a note to Jonah, but I thought that might be a little weird. He also suggested thanking him during lunch break, but I thought I would be even more shy with other kids around us. Finally, he suggested a solution I really liked. "Since Ruth and Jonah are in your math group, maybe you can decide on something to tell both of them during your work in math class."

"I like that idea! But what should I say?"

"Let's see," Dad said. "What do you want to say to them?"

Well, I wanted to say that I really appreciated them standing up to Danny during yesterday's lunch break, and that it really made me feel better.

"Well, why don't you say just that?" Dad said.

"You're right! That's what I'll say."

"Mom, isn't it cool that my friends were really excited about plants?"

"Yes! That's amazing! I think it was the spark in your eyes when you told them about it that really did it," she said smiling.

"You said you'd tell me about plant embryos," I added.

"Yes, my love, I can tell you more about plants if you want."

"I do, tell me, but only the cool stuff!" I said, because I don't always like it when she gets into the details.

"OK, let's start with embryos. I brought something to show you." She pulled a small clear tube out of her jeans pocket. "Are these seeds?" I asked her.

"Yes, these are Arabidopsis seeds," she said.

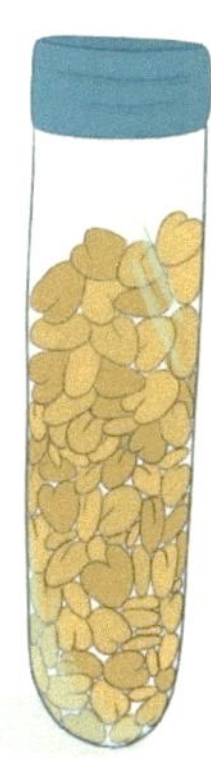

"So, this is where Arbi came from!" I sat up pointing to the pot on my desk.

"Right. I seeded Arbi for you in the soil. Plant seeds are super unique, because they have an embryo inside them with a small root and shoot and the meristem, but they need to be kept extremely dry." Mom pointed at the tube of seeds as she was speaking.

"They don't die?" I got worried.

“That is the cool part”, Mom said. “While most plants would die if they got extremely dry, most seeds are able to maintain the full plant potential within them during extreme dehydration. Once you water them, the embryo inside the seed starts growing, rupturing the seed coat, and growing into a seedling.”

“Then after they emerge from the soil with their apical hook, the meristem grows more and more leaves?” I wanted to make sure I created a correct image in my mind.

“Yes, exactly like that,” Mom confirmed.

“How is a flower formed? Is that also from the meristem? How does the meristem know when to make a leaf and when to make a flower?”

"Those are brilliant questions, my smart daughter, but it's pretty late now, and it's reading time." Mom handed over my book and gave me a kiss on my forehead. "Good night, my sweetheart, sweet dreams."

She walked out of my room, and I opened my book. While I was reading, I was imagining the meristem creating leaves and flowers, like in an animated cartoon.

Chapter 5: Encountering Stress

The next morning on the kitchen counter I saw a note from my mother who had already left for work. The note said:

My dear Lona,

Asking questions is one of the most important things in life. Here is the question we left unanswered yesterday, "How is a flower formed?" Let's get back to it when we meet this afternoon. Have a happy day.

Love you,

Mom

The only thing Mom did not take into consideration was that Ruth was coming over right after gymnastics. Oh wait, maybe she would actually be interested in this, as well!

After gymnastics, I'm usually starving, so I asked Mom if she could take Ruth and me for i-Scream on the way home. Luckily, she agreed!

We stopped at iScream, my favorite ice cream shop. They have the best toppings, like white chocolate and star-shaped sparkles. We got cones and brought one home for my little sister, Eli.

iScream
OPEN

We arrived home, and Eli jumped for joy when I gave her the ice cream.

"Do you want to see Arbi?" I asked Ruth.

"Sure," said Ruth. We went up the stairs to my room, and there she was.

I was shocked.

"MOM!" I shouted.

Mom came running up. "What happened?"
"Arbi is suffering!" I said, worried.

"I see," said Mom. "Arbi got a little bit dehydrated. It was a warm day. Bring a glass of water, Lona. Let's water the soil."
I ran down and filled a glass with water and then

slowly headed back to my room and handed the glass to my mother.

She handed the glass back to me and said, “Go ahead, you can water her. Just until the soil is saturated with water.”

I added the water to Arbi’s pot while Mom tried to calm me down: “Arbi will be OK. Plants know how to cope with stress. Stress and recovery are an inevitable part of their lives.”

Stress? What did she mean by stress? Plants are stressed? I was surprised.

“Are they worried they will be late to school, too?” Ruth asked, joking.

We were all laughing now.

"Yes, plants encounter stress all throughout their lives," said Mom.

"What kind of stress?" asked Ruth, and I felt some confusion in her voice.

"What kind of stress do you think plants face?" Mom asked, training us as amateur investigators.

After thinking for a while, Ruth said, "No water?"

"Right!" said Mom, "Water stress. Without water, plants will wilt and dry out. What other stress types can you think of?"

"Crush stress?" I tried.

"Yes, of course, that is a stress as well. People can just move, but plants can't. They stay in the same place. Plants can't go get water elsewhere. They can't hide from strong rainfall or animals walking on them," Mom said.

"So, what DO they do when they face those problems?" I wondered.

"That is a great question," Mom said. "But I owe you an answer from yesterday."

"What was the question?" Ruth jumped in.

"How do plants flower?" I replied.

Chapter 6: The Meristem

"You know," Mom said, "I think this is one of the most fascinating questions in plant biology. Actually, a lot about this process has already been discovered."

"Do you remember that I told you about the meristem? So, there are actually two meristems in Arabidopsis. Arbi has a shoot apical meristem between her leaves, and a root apical meristem at the tip of her root. The

SHOOT
APICAL MERISTEM
ROOT
APICAL MERISTEM

meristem is a group of cells that can make new cells and create new organs." Mom paused to make sure we were both following.

I jumped off my bed and ran toward Arbi to try and see the meristem.

"Mom, can you show us the meristem?" Mom and Ruth came over to my desk, where Arbi was placed in her pot.

"One of the downsides of Arabidopsis is that they are too small to easily see the meristem without a microscope," Mom said.

"So, let's go to your laboratory to see it under the microscope!" I said.

"Yes, let's go!" Ruth agreed.

"It's too late to go to the laboratory right now, but we can do it some other day."

Ruth and I sighed in slight disappointment.

"But anyway", Mom continued, "at a certain point in time, which is usually measured by a certain number of leaves that the meristem has created, Arbi will bolt."

"Bolt?" I interrupted Mom's description.

"Right, bolting means developing a long stem that grows away from the soil, and on which the inflorescence and flowers will form."

"I can't wait to see Arbi bolting!" I said. "Wait, is that how you use that word?" We all laughed.

"Yes, soon Arbi will start bolting, depending on the number of light hours during the day and her age."

LONG-DAY GROWTH SHORT-DAY GROWTH

A knock on the door interrupted our discussion. It was Ruth's dad. Ruth and I ran down the stairs, and I opened the door.

"Hello Mr. Brown," I said. "Please come in." Ruth grabbed her dad's hand and dragged him in, saying, "yes, Daddy, come hear about how plants grow. It's so cool!"

Mr. Brown scrunched his eyebrows. He looked surprised to see Ruth excited about plants. "We have to go home for dinner, honey. Mommy is waiting for us. Why don't you tell me all about it on the way home?" Mr. Brown said, picking Ruth up in his arms.

Ruth hugged her dad and pushed herself back down. "Thank you, Ms. Williams. I'll see you tomorrow, Lona. Don't forget to tell me how plants flower!"

Mom and I smiled, and while I gave Ruth a hug, Mom looked at Mr. Brown and then at Ruth and said, "It is always a pleasure having you over, Ruth."

Eli was again helping Dad make dinner, so the vegetables were cut less elegantly than usual, but, since I didn't help make dinner, I didn't complain about it.

After we finished eating our veggies, Dad brought over a mushroom casserole he made, which my mom was crazy about. Mom got all excited and asked if there was any of that spicy sauce left that she brought from Japan.

As part of her work as a plant scientist, Mom has conferences she goes to all around the world. We get presents from the coolest places. Last year she went to Paris and Australia, and a few weeks ago she returned from a conference in Japan.

My sister and I both agreed that presents from Japan were the most unique!

Chapter 7: A Brave Heart

On a sunny Sunday morning Eli and I made breakfast together. We decided to make pancakes with Mom's help. While I was pouring the pancake mixture on the frying pan, I recalled that I still didn't know how plants create flowers from the meristem and noted to myself that this would be the next thing I would ask Mom.

Cooper started jumping in front of the door to let us know he wanted to go to the park.

I opened the garage door and was met by

a strong smell of laundry freshness. I headed over to the shelf where we keep all our pool toys, and there was a paper bag with Cooper's new toy from Japan. It was a toy the size of a tennis ball with handles we can hold and throw for Cooper to fetch. I grabbed the purple toy and yelled over to Dad, "Let's go to the park with Cooper!"

Dad asked Eli and Mom if they wanted to come, and we all went together.

It was late morning on a Sunday, so there were many dogs at the park. Some children were playing in the playground, and I spotted Alaina, a friend from class. I handed the ball over to Dad and said that I was going to say hello to Alaina.

"Alaina!" I shouted when I got closer to the swings where she was playing with her younger brother.

"Hi Lona!" A big smile spread over Alaina's face as she ran toward me. We chit-chatted, completely neglecting Alaina's five-year-old brother on the swings. We climbed together to the top of the playground bridge and sat down there. We talked about our graduation play as we observed the occurrences from above.

Suddenly, we heard someone crying.

At the beginning we ignored the noise, but then I saw Alaina's brother crying with all his heart. We both jumped up and ran over toward the swings. Alaina hugged her little brother and asked, "What happened, Maxi?"

Max, still gasping, pointed at a girl playing by the swings. Once we were able to calm Max down, he told us, with his very cute voice, that this girl told him that her parents say if you swing too much, you get nightmares. Then he resumed his passionate crying. Alaina hugged Max again. "Maxi," she said with a compassionate voice, "that girl just wanted to get the swing and tried to scare you, so you would get down and she could take over."

While I was listening to their conversation, I felt like someone should tell that girl she could have simply asked instead of making up a scary story. I was a bit hesitant; she looked kind of mean. Then, I remembered how I felt when my friends stood up for me, and I decided this was a small event to practice on. I interrupted Alaina and asked Max if he wanted to come with me to talk to that girl. He said no.

I went over to the girl, and said "Hi. I'm Lona, and that little guy there, Max, is my friend's little brother. Did you tell him that too much swinging makes nightmares?" She ignored me.

"Hey," I said.

She turned her head toward me. "Yes."

"I understand," I said, feeling like my mom, "but you know that really scared him. Instead, you could have just told him you wanted to swing." My heart was pounding, but at the same time I felt an interesting feeling: I think it felt like being brave.

"Sorry," she said, not super convincingly, and skipped away from the playground. I stood there for a minute to think about that conversation. It felt good to say things as they are. I walked over to Alaina and Max. Max looked at me with watery eyes. I smiled at him warmly and said, "She said she is sorry about that. There won't be any nightmares for swinging too much."

While I was playing with Alaina at the playground, Mom had already returned home and started preparing dinner. She set carrot sticks, red pepper triangles, and radish spirals for us to use in our veggie mandala. I felt strong and inspired and was ready to get creative with my veggies.

After dinner, we decided to have a dance party. Each of us picked a song, and we all danced together in the living room. Eli chose a hip hop song, so we both did our hip hop class dance. I don't want to even talk about how Mom and Dad danced to that song. It was so funny! Mom chose music suitable for contemporary dancing. Then we all danced with slower moves, lifting one leg high, taking it down slowly, while lifting one arm slowly to the sky. Dad was hilarious, trying to imitate us with these slow movements.

We ended the dance party on the floor laughing so hard with our legs in the air, until our abdominal muscles hurt.

Chapter 8: The Flower Whorls

Sometimes I don't like going to sleep by myself and prefer Mom or Dad to tell me a story. Today was one of those days. "Mom, will you tell me how plants flower?"

"Of course, my love, but first, did you water Arbi recently?" Mom was right. I forgot to water Arbi.

I took the glass that I left on my desk and filled it with water from the bathroom. I added some water to Arbi, so that the soil was moist but not flooded. I got back in bed, and Mom sat beside me. "Do you remember what bolting is?"

"I don't remember," I said.

"Bolting is when a long stem grows from the Arabidopsis leaves. We will soon see Arbi bolting."

I was excited! "When will that happen?"

"Well, that depends. Plants really interact with their environment," Mom said. "Arabidopsis can look very different based on the number of light or dark hours it is exposed to or changes in temperature."

"Like really different? How different?" I asked.

"Well, when the days are shorter in winter, Arbi will make about 50 leaves before bolting and flowering. In the summer when there are more light hours in a day, it can flower after making just 12 or so leaves. So then, the plants in winter look much bushier with many more leaves."

"But why? What causes this difference?" I wanted to understand better.

"There is a signal inside the plant that tells it that it's time to bolt, and then the meristem becomes an inflorescence meristem."

"Wait, Mom, what does that mean? I got confused."

"It means that, instead of making leaf

cells, it starts making flower cells to create the flowers."

"Oh, I get it. So, some signal in the plant tells the meristem to change, like pushing a button."

"It's exactly like that," Mom reassured me.

"And then the meristem starts creating Arabidopsis flowers?"

"Yes, from the meristem the flower will form with cells of different flower whorls."

"What are whorls?" I asked.

"Whorls are the different layers of the flower. You know how roses have colorful and sometimes fragrant petals?"

"Oh, yeah, I know petals, but what are other whorls?" I asked.

"Sepals are the green, leaf-like layer outside the petals, and inside the flowers there are also stamens and carpels. The stamens usually have yellow powder, and the carpel is the most inner layer in the flowers." Mom answered my question thoroughly.

"So, there are four whorls? I want to make sure I got that right."

"Correct, four whorls: sepals, petals, stamens, and carpel. That is from the outside-inward." Mom reassured me. "It's now time for bed."

A yawn washed over me. “Just one last thing, Mom. What are the stamens and carpel for?”

“The stamen and carpel are the reproductive tissues of the plant. It means that with these two tissues the plant will make new seeds.”

“The reproductive tissue, like you and Dad making Eli and me?”

“Exactly. Just some plants, like Arbi, can do it all on their own. Arbi has all she needs to make her own baby seeds.”

Mom got up, gave me a good night kiss, and said, “Good night, darling.”

I turned off the small light by my bed and just before I fell asleep, I imagined Arbi shooting her stem up to the sky and bolting.

Chapter 9: Recovery

On the next weekend we took a road trip to Grandma's house. I asked Mom if I should take Arbi with us, so that she wouldn't get dry and wilt. Mom said that, if I leave Arbi with some water in a plate under the pot, she should survive the weekend. I found a small plate with high edges, moisturized the soil, and added water to the plate below the pot.

It was Sunday evening when we arrived back home. It was already dark, and Eli fell asleep on the way, like always. Dad carried her up to bed, and I took her bag and mine up to my room. I turned on the lights and started unpacking my bag. Fortunately, most of my clothes were dirty, which made it easy to just throw all of them in the laundry basket. When I turned back toward my bag, I noticed something different out of the corner of my eye. I lifted my gaze to my desk, and there it was.

"Arbi has bolted! Mom!" I shouted.

"Shhhh..." Mom said, "Eli's asleep."

There it was, with a still-tiny but very visible stem elongated over her leaves. I was genuinely enthusiastic to see Arbi changing her shape, growing longer, maturing toward her next stage in life, preparing for flowering.

"When will we see her flowers, Mom?"

"Probably in the next few days, my dear. Let's get ready for bed."

The next morning as I was getting ready for school, I noticed Arbi's stem had gotten a bit taller. I thought that I would see her flowers very soon. I was very curious to see what her flowers would look like.

It was an extremely hot day. When we returned home after school, the house was still very warm from the heat of the day. I went upstairs to my room to change into my gymnastics outfit.

While I was changing, I looked at Arbi. Something looked wrong. I finished getting dressed and came closer to get a better look. I saw that some of Arbi's leaves had brownish spots on their edges, like they were burned or dried up.

I was worried. The soil in Arbi's pot was dry. I immediately added water. Mom wasn't back from work yet, so I couldn't ask her to take a look and reassure me that Arbi was going to be OK. I remember Mom telling me about how plants know how to deal with stress. The extreme heat we had was probably stressful for Arbi. I wondered if this was a stress Arbi could get over, since her leaves looked really damaged, and I was worried I wouldn't get to see her flowers.

I sat there in my room as time passed by, thinking about what could help Arbi overcome this damage.

Eli came over to my room and asked if she could try on my dresses. I agreed, and she started making a mess in my room. It makes her so happy when I agree, and the truth is, I was distracted, so I just said yes without paying much attention.

Mom arrived and came up to my room. She smiled, looking at Eli enjoying herself swirling right and left in one of my dresses. "What's wrong, Lona?"

"I'm OK," I said, "It's Arbi."

"I see. It's probably the heat," Mom said, hovering over my desk looking closely at Arbi.

"That's what I thought. Can she recover?" I worried.

"I think so, but we will need to give her a few days, and maybe you should take her down to the kitchen. It's not so warm there during the daytime."

"Mom, how can plants recover from all the stress? They get dry, overheated, and you said there are even more kinds of stress."

"Yes, there is also cold and freeze stress, wounding, and also insects that can harm plants."

"So how is it possible that they survive all these problems even without being able to run away or fight back?"

“They do fight back. Plants have many ways to handle these problems. I can give you a cool example regarding light. Plants need light in order to grow, and if there is not enough light, that could be considered a problem for them. Sometimes plants grow close to each other, and some plants hover over another plant and shade it, preventing sufficient light exposure to the lower plant.”

“Oh I see, yes, so what does the lower plant do? Can it move the higher plant shading it?”

“Not really, but it can do something really clever. The lower plant, with not enough light, will change its growing program and elongate its stem to get over the leaves blocking the light. That way it is exposed to the sunlight again and can go back to normal growth.”

"That is SO COOL! What else? How do plants recover from drying?"

"Oh!" said Mom, "That's my favorite question, girl! That is my actual research question at work."

"Really?"

"Yes, really. We don't know a lot about

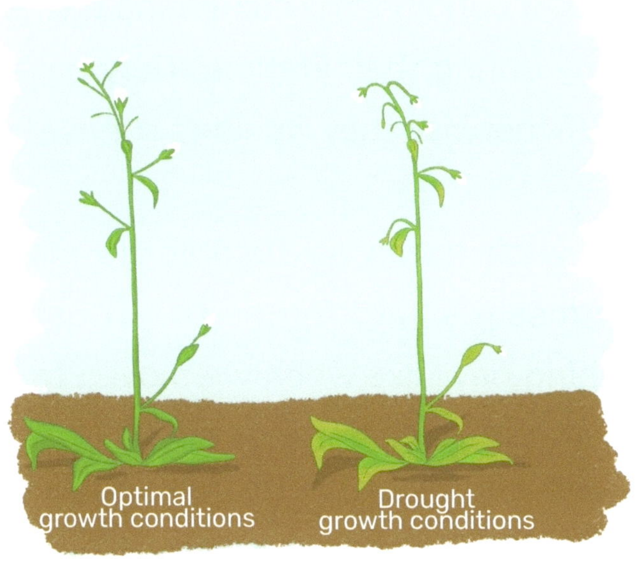

how plants recover from stress. There are still many unanswered questions about plants, and we are working toward finding the answers."

"But I want to know!" I urged her to give me an answer, unsatisfied with her response.

"I am doing my best so that I can soon give you a clear answer on that, but we still have a way to go. I can tell you though that adapting to different conditions is something plants do regularly during their lifetime. They have no choice. Otherwise they wouldn't survive."

"I wish I was as flexible as plants. Sometimes it's hard for me to get used to something new, like when we moved to San Diego, and I didn't know anybody."

"That's right, love, we also face changes in our lives." Mom looked at me, and we both knew that she was thinking about her parents, Grandma and Grandpa, who she really missed since we moved to San Diego.

"But the faster we adapt and get used to the new environment, even if that means making small alterations in the way we used to live before, the faster we can get back to enjoying the moment," she said.

Chapter 10: Green Beginnings

I sat in the garden daydreaming, while Cooper was jumping around me, urging me to play with him. I thought about how weird it was when I first moved to San Diego for Mom's new job as a plant biology researcher. It was weird, because I didn't know anybody or any place. Everything was new. But as time went by, I felt more and more at home here. I established a group of good friends, met my best friend

Ruth, and even found a secret crush, that I will definitely not share with you!

I thought about how amazing plants are with their ability to constantly face challenges they can't run away from, and how they need to find ways to overcome every problem they face. As I was feeling inspired by all the plants surrounding me in our garden, Eli came running out with Arbi's pot.

"Look, Lona, Arbi made flowers!" I hopped up from the chair to take a close look. Arbi had several tiny flowers with white petals, which I tried smelling. They had no scent, but they were lovely. I knew Arbi was completing the whole life cycle, from the tiny seed it germinated out of entering the world, humbled, with her stem bent, leaves pointing downward, and spreading them wide open as they burst from the soil to face the sun. She would soon have all her flowers blooming with joy and would finally create many of her own little seeds.

I had it all planned out. I would collect Arbi's seeds and grow 24 seedlings in individual pots. That will be my graduation gift for each of my classmates. Yes, even including Danny.

I smiled to myself, thinking of all my friends carrying home a tiny pot with a green beginning.

I want to thank:

Assif Eliaz, Ofer Afik, Ada Li, and Eilon Eliaz for your smart suggestions. Your comments have helped improve this book from a child's perspective, which is the most important one in this case!

Sandee Illouz and Nirit Wigdor for reviewing and giving insightful comments.

Arbi
Arbi
Arbi
Arbi
Arbi
Arbi
Arbi
Arbi

Hello hello!

If you made it to this point, I suspect that you are a curious kid, like me!

These empty lines are for you to write down exciting new things you learn.

What did you hear lately that made you want to learn more about?

Note things you find yourself curious about and add information you learn about those things.

Remember- each one of us is curious about different things, and that's the beauty of it - learn about what YOU are curious and passionate about. And... Enjoy!

Yours truly,

Lona

If you are super curious about plants and have any questions, please send them my way! You can email your questions to me at eliaz.nat@gmail.com

www.ingramcontent.com/pod-product-compliance
Ingram Content Group UK Ltd.
Pitfield, Milton Keynes, MK11 3LW, UK
UKHW060404300726
14090UKWH00006B/429